My Mended HEART

Micah N. Dillon

For more information, please visit
www.sendingandmending.com

To contact Micah and/or inquire about speaking, email
micahmendedheart@gmail.com

Published by The Core Media Group, Inc., P.O. Box 2037, Indian Trail, NC 28079

Cover and Interior Design: Ashlyn Helms

ISBN: 978-1-950465-35-4

Printed in the United States of America.

I would like to dedicate this book to my loving husband of 13 years, Benjamin Stevan Dillon. Thank you for the unconditional love you gave to me and everyone you encountered. It has been said everyone felt you were their best friend. You would be happy to know all of those best friends have reciprocated your many acts of kindness back to me and the kids. To you, I will always be grateful. For you were the closest example of Jesus that I have experienced on earth. I cannot wait to embrace you in heaven.

Acknowledgements

My two wonderful children, Stone and Stella:

You are my sunshine and my drive to be "the more" God has called me to be. Know you are my best gift and I cherish you every day as you bring me endless joy. I love you Stone and Stella, now and forever.

My Family:

I have been shown love, strength, and the power of prayer throughout my life. Thank you for believing in me, for standing with me, and for encouraging me to follow after Jesus, my true source. Thank you for teaching me to hunger for the presence of God and to worship Him in an authentic way.

The Dillon Family:

"For wherever you go, I will go; And wherever you lodge, I will lodge; Your people shall be my people, And your God, my God."
Ruth 1:16 NKJV

These were the vows I spoke on June 5, 2004, and have stood by ever since. When Ben passed, I made this statement, "I might have gotten here because of my last name, but I'm not staying here because of it." I made a choice right then and there that this goes beyond my last name. WE ARE FAMILY! Eternal rewards come to those who can see past the natural realm and into the spiritual. The covenant I made with your family was eternal; and for that I am forever grateful.

My Rock Church Family:

Thank you for showing me what a local church body can do when you put faith into action. I have experienced the presence of God in a greater measure as we have worshipped together. Grieving together made everything better. Thank you for believing in miracles with me. We will continue to hold on to His promises.

The Franklin, Virginia Community:

I am proud to be a part of a community that shows up for people. You have taught me that we are better together. We can go further, longer, and stronger when we are together. Thank you for all the hometown goodness.

A Note to the Reader

My prayer is that this book will impact you and allow you to find the Great Mender of all, Jesus, as I have. He mended my heart for a better tomorrow, and He will do the same for you, my friend.

How many of us have perceptions of who others are—without actually asking them how they came to be? How many of us assume we know other people's stories—not because we've asked them, but because we've made those stories up in our own heads?

How many of us do that with God?

***

On November 12, 2016, I went to a concert—a night of worship hosted by Cory Asbury, Amanda Cook and Steffany

Gretzinger of Bethel Music at Regent University in Virginia Beach, Virginia. I joined in from the audience as they sang the beautiful words to "King of My Heart."

I can't really describe it, but something happened inside of me during that song. The atmosphere shifted. I felt the overwhelming presence of God. The Lord deposited something in my heart that night—something directly from Him. A direct, mysterious impartation.

Four months later, in April 2017, I attended another concert—Jonathan David and Melissa Helser of Bethel Music at Rock Church International, founded by John and Anne Gimenez. At the end of the concert, my husband's longtime friend and worship leader, Joy, approached me and said, out of the blue: "You need to get out of your head, Micah. You need to start writing music." Another seemingly serendipitous encounter from above.

Two days after that, lyrics came into my mind. All of a sudden, I had this song from God:

I look to you for help
For the pressure of this life bears down on me
I look to you for help
So, let your presence come and blow through me
Let your presence come until I am free

For the joy of the Lord renews my strength

I named it "Joy of the Lord," and started preparing it for our church's annual anniversary service—the church where I've led worship for the past four years. And during the anniversary service that June, I led our congregation in worship with that song.

Two days later, on June 12, 2017—seven months to the day after that concert at Regent University—I woke up on that Monday morning to find Ben, my husband of 13 years, unconscious in the shower. At 43 years old, in good health, Ben Dillon died of a heart attack—the "widowmaker," as doctors called it. At 36, mother to two young children, Stone (7) and Stella (5), I now had to continue life without my husband.

In almost an instant, I lost three key aspects of my identity. After 13 years of marriage, I was no longer a wife. After 15 years of growing my real estate business, I stepped away from my career to take care of Stone and Stella. On top of that, I temporarily lost my ability to sing because of overuse. For six months, everything I relied upon for identity, purpose and worth was stripped away. In those months, I realized the only identity that truly matters is my identity as a child of God.

Yet, in the middle of that time, God provided *Himself* to fill in the gaps of my life.

Songs like "King of My Heart," "You Came (Lazarus)" and "The Future Marches In" began to speak overwhelming truth into my life. The Word of God came alive within my soul; I began to see Him in the trees, in the wind, in the sunsets. As I prayed specific prayers, creation became evidence of the Father's nearness through feathers, fireflies, dolphins, and eagles. Like that mysterious encounter at the Bethel night of worship, God began to reveal Himself to me in new, fresh and powerful ways.

His loving kindness is all around us. Through every battle, He's in control.

During the past three years, God has given words and

inspiration like this to encourage me and others. In the midst of that, He encouraged me to surrender and become obedient to those good thoughts. I wrote them down in my journal, and through this book, I'm sharing them in the hope that others might be encouraged and filled with the joy of the Lord. Ultimately, I just want to give God credit for the good thoughts He has imparted to me. Every good thought is a God thought. It's God, the Divine Encourager, the Holy Spirit, prompting us toward good things.

By the grace of God, as I surrendered to Him and His goodness, He allowed me to lead Ben's funeral service—overflowing with 800-plus people from across the country—in worship to "The Joy of the Lord." Because of the Lord's great mercy and grace, He shared those beautiful words He'd given to me with a crowd of worshipers mourning the loss of my husband:

So, let your presence come and blow through me
Let your presence come until I am free

For the joy of the Lord renews my strength

Since that Monday morning in June, I've been on a journey to know the Father's heart and understand His nature. For too long, I assumed I knew my Creator; I built the story of God and His character in my head without actually seeking and surrendering to Him. Now, through this book and the powerful words of Scripture, I'm inviting you to join me on this journey to discover the One who created us, knows us and lives inside of us.

"The more I know God, the more I desire to be with Him. His presence overcomes everything."

"I have found the gateway to God, the pathway to his presence for all his lovers."
Psalm 118:20 TPT

"God's empowering presence brings His presents into our lives. The more I'm saturated by His presence, the more confident I grow in His gifts of faith, hope and love."

"Until then, there are three things that remain: faith, hope, and love—yet love surpasses them all. So, above all else, let love be the beautiful prize for which you run."
1 Corinthians 13:13 TPT

"The freedom for which we pray won't come until we surrender the disappointments of our past. Letting go of yesterday allows space in your heart for the gains of tomorrow."

"The things that distinguish a true apostle were performed among you with great perseverance—supernatural signs, startling wonders, and awesome miracles."
2 Corinthians 12:12 TPT

"Fear takes us to places we don't need to go. Faith in Jesus takes us to places we never dreamed we could go."

"But we are certainly not those who are held back by fear and perish; we are among those who have faith and experience true life!"
Hebrews 10:39 TPT

"Keep the garden of your heart pure. Don't let attitudes of bitterness and self-hatred enter. Keep it spotless. Keep the weeds out. How? Connect with Jesus. He will communicate back to you when you are open to hear and trust. His words will be kind, gentle and convicting. His conviction illuminates the lies behind the surface of our hearts. To live a life of freedom, you have to uncover the lies influencing your daily decisions. It hurts at first, but joy comes in the morning every single time."

"Before I confessed my sins, I kept it all inside; my dishonesty devastated my inner life, causing my life to be filled with frustration, irrepressible anguish, and misery. The pain never let up, for your hand of conviction was heavy on my heart. My strength was sapped, my inner life dried up like a spiritual drought within my soul. *Pause in his presence.* Then I finally admitted to you all my sins, refusing to hide them any longer. I said, "My life-giving God, I will openly acknowledge my evil actions." And you forgave me! All at once the guilt of my sin washed away and all my pain disappeared! Pause in his presence"

Psalm 32:3-5 TPT

"Surrender your story for His glory."

"Laying your life down in tender surrender before the Lord will bring life, prosperity, and honor as your reward."
Proverbs 22:4 TPT

"In the sending comes the mending. What encouraging word can you send someone today?"

"I tell you the truth, whoever accepts anyone I send also accepts me. And whoever accepts me also accepts the One who sent me.""
John 13:20 NCV

"With humble confidence, Jesus wants us to dig deep into the roots of Faith. There you will find nine fruits: love, joy, peace, patience, kindness, goodness, faithfulness, gentleness and self-control."

"But the fruit produced by the Holy Spirit within you is divine love in all its varied expressions: joy that overflows, peace that subdues, patience that endures, kindness in action, a life full of virtue, faith that prevails, gentleness of heart, and strength of spirit. Never set the law above these qualities, for they are meant to be limitless."
Galatians 5:22-23 TPT

"We all need to overcome obstacles to get closer to Jesus, but we can't do this in isolation. Who do you know at their breaking point? Who can you pray for today? Are you at your breaking point? Encourage each other to push through the obstacles. You will find Jesus waiting for you on the other side."

"This is why I wait upon you, expecting your breakthrough, for your word brings me hope."
Psalm 130:5 TPT

"How are you carrying God's presence? Is His presence inside of us, even if it's just a small seed? Is it staying small or is it growing? How we carry God's presence will determine if a season of growth will come. We have to steward the seed, nurture it. Dropping the seed into the soil isn't enough. We need to check on it, fertilize it, water it, and pull weeds out of it. Neglect will kill the seed. Salvation is the seed, but what happens after is on us. Take the first steps toward your future destiny."

"The seed sown among weeds represents the person who receives the message, but all of life's busy distractions, his divided heart, and his ambition for wealth result in suffocating the kingdom message and prevent him from bearing spiritual fruit. As for the seed that fell upon good, rich soil, it represents the hearts of people who hear and fully embrace the message of heaven's kingdom realm. Their lives bear good fruit—some yield a harvest of thirty, sixty, even one hundred times as much as was sown."

Matthew 13:22-23 TPT

"You are never alone in Jesus. Never doubt you are protected under the shadow of His wings. His love for you is everlasting!"

"His massive arms are wrapped around you, protecting you. You can run under his covering of majesty and hide. His arms of faithfulness are a shield keeping you from harm."
Psalm 91:4 TPT

"Small acts of obedience will build Jesus into every fiber of our being."

"This is how we can be sure that we love the children of God: by having a passionate love for God and by obedience to his commands."
1 John 5:2 TPT

"The journey can be exhausting, lonely, and challenging. When you are too tired to know how or what to pray, know this: Jesus knows your heart and is your advocate to the Father. He will never leave you or forget you."

"And in a similar way, the Holy Spirit takes hold of us in our human frailty to empower us in our weakness. For example, at times we don't even know how to pray, or know the best things to ask for. But the Holy Spirit rises up within us to super-intercede on our behalf, pleading to God with emotional sighs too deep for words."
Romans 8:26 TPT

"Jesus will bring people into your life to help heal the wounded places in your heart. When you are ready, you will find them; you will find a piece of Jesus in everyone you meet."

"He heals the wounds of every shattered heart."
Psalm 147:3 TPT

"When you start your day with a thankful heart, everything else follows that gratitude. Take a walk and look for God's loving kindness all around you. The more you see His kindness, the more you believe in His kindness toward you. The more you believe it, the more you receive it. The more you receive it, the more of His kindness you have to give away."

"At each and every sunrise we will be thanking
you for your kindness and your love. As the
sun sets and all through the night, we will keep
proclaiming, 'You are so faithful!'"
Psalm 92:2 TPT

"When you have Jesus as a friend, He adds more to your life. Embrace His 'more' in your life every day. You are always more than enough. You always have more than enough, and you never know who needs the 'more' you have found."

"The Lord is my best friend and my shepherd.
I always have more than enough."
Psalm 23:1 TPT

"Be a messenger to others. Give a good word—it may just change a life."

"Anxious fear brings depression, but a life-giving word of encouragement can do wonders to restore joy to the heart."
Proverbs 12:25 TPT

"When the days ahead feel like dread, take a look in the beautiful Word of God. One bite at a time, you'll find it only takes faith the size of a mustard seed to grow for all to see. In the moment, it may not seem like much, but looking back, you'll say, 'hip hip hurray! I've grown today.'"

"Then Jesus taught them another parable: 'Heaven's kingdom realm can be compared to the tiny mustard seed that a man takes and plants in his field. Although the smallest of all the seeds, it eventually grows into the greatest of garden plants, becoming a tree for birds to come and build their nests in its branches.'"
Matthew 13:31-32 TPT

"When you're growing, you start a-glowing."

"All your promises glow with fire; that's why I'm a lover of your word."
Psalm 119:140 TPT

"A full life is about discovering more than just the secrets within; it's about discovering the secrets of men. When you read the Bible, it reads you back. It's the living, breathing Spirit Word. The more the Holy Spirit connects to our spirit, the more the mysteries are unlocked. Revelation is only found in a heart hungry for truth. Ask for eyes that see the miracles that so many miss. God grants the desires of a heart aligned with His."

"Such amazing mysteries found within every miracle that nearly everyone seems to miss. Those with no discernment can never really discover the deep and glorious secrets hidden in your ways."
Psalm 92:6 TPT

"Reconciliation is a bridge with love in between us."

"In other words, it was through the Anointed One that God was shepherding the world, not even keeping records of their transgressions, and he has entrusted to us the ministry of opening the door of reconciliation to God."
2 Corinthians 5:19 TPT

"We worship Jesus not just as a body of believers, but as body-builders—building the body of Christ up, together, from strength to strength to withstand the challenges ahead."

"God has given me unique gifts as a skilled master builder who lays a good foundation. Afterward another craftsman comes and builds on it. So, builders beware! Let every builder do his work carefully, according to God's standards."
1 Corinthians 3:10 TPT

"Remember to praise the people in your life. Build others up with your words and deeds. Show up for them and support them, because our God is our strength."

"Your praise to God is admirable, but it does nothing to strengthen and build up others."
1 Corinthians 14:17 TPT

"May our strength be the love we have for one another."

"And to love Him with all the heart, with all the understanding, with all the soul, and with all the strength, and to love one's neighbor as oneself, is more than all the whole burnt offerings and sacrifices."
Mark 12:33 NKJV

“So many people are known by their negative experiences, but our identity does not need to be tied to our traumas. When life blindsides us, we have a choice as to how we respond. Refuse to be the victim. Injustice happens every day, but when I decided to use my voice and listen to my heart instead of making excuses for my lack of response, I was able to connect to the true power source. Courage woke up. Confidence started to build. Peace was accessible. The power is closer than you think. Once you access the freedom, your common story turns into an uncommon story. Use your voice to tell your story. He gets the glory for every uncommon story.”

“Stop imitating the ideals and opinions of the culture around you, but be inwardly transformed by the Holy Spirit through a total reformation of how you think. This will empower you to discern God’s will as you live a beautiful life, satisfying and perfect in his eyes.”

Romans 12:2 TPT

"When we store up God's Word and goodness deep within our souls, we can serve and help restore others with the gift of reconciliation through His Spirit."

"People are known in this same way. Out of the virtue stored in their hearts, good and upright people will produce good fruit. But out of the evil hidden in their hearts, evil ones will produce what is evil. For the overflow of what has been stored in your heart will be seen by your fruit and will be heard in your words."
Luke 6:45 TPT

"Forgiveness is one of the best gifts you can give someone. Forgiveness takes courage— let go of the fault you have in your heart toward another person and reopen the door to a true relationship."

"Tolerate the weaknesses of those in the family of faith, forgiving one another in the same way you have been graciously forgiven by Jesus Christ. If you find fault with someone, release this same gift of forgiveness to them."
Colossians 3:13 TPT

"Part of restoring and healing our hearts is allowing God to show up in our plans. Embrace it and see His manifestation in your life."

"May God give you every desire of your heart and carry out your every plan as you go to battle."
Psalm 20:4 TPT

"Some trust in the work they do. Some trust in material wealth. I choose to trust in the name of Yahweh, the Lord our God. It's a name worth more than everything. His love never fails. His name always prevails. Trust in His name."

"Some trust in chariots, and some in horses; But we will remember the name of the LORD our God."
Psalm 20:7 NKJV

"Comparison kills us. It tears us down. When what someone else has becomes the focus of our affections, we give permission to the Enemy to deceive us. We start to believe we've fallen short. That we're failing. That we're missing something. The unchanging truth is we are fearfully, wonderfully and uniquely made. Your journey is your journey. You are a child of the King, so stay in your lane with your eyes on your future. When you connect inward, it will propel you forward."

"I will praise You, for I am fearfully and wonderfully made; Marvelous are Your works, and that my soul knows very well."
Psalm 139:14 NKJV

"A life of surrender allows God into our mundane lives. Do we trust in our Maker? Are we asking God, 'Where is your assignment for me today?', 'Who am I here for today?' and 'Who can I bless?' This is when the mundane becomes magnificent."

"Then you will be God's servant, fully mature and perfectly prepared to fulfill any assignment God gives you."
2 Timothy 3:17 TPT

"His kindness allows us to feel His presence as we navigate through disappointment and rejection. When life turns into a treasure hunt, you will find that He is the ultimate prize. May this cause a prayer to rise up, saying, "Jesus be the treasure of my heart. I forgot You are enough, but I remember now."

"Lord, I have chosen you alone as my inheritance. You are my prize, my pleasure, and my portion. I leave my destiny and its timing in your hands."
Psalm 16:5 TPT

"When hearts are surrendered, joy starts to rise. In His presence, hope comes alive. Your heart starts to sing, 'Let me go, let me go. Just one step at a time.' The next thing you know, you'll hear yourself say, 'I didn't know I would find You, but I found You. Yes, I found You.'"

"Here's the one thing I crave from God, the one thing I seek above all else: I want the privilege of living with him every moment in his house, finding the sweet loveliness of his face, filled with awe, delighting in his glory and grace. I want to live my life so close to him that he takes pleasure in my every prayer."
Psalm 27:4 TPT

"Our hearts are like a house. So many see the exterior and perceive it's happy inside, but often times our closets are full of junk. Our attic is full of junk. Until we are willing to open the closets and attics of our heart, we will never be fully clean, fully known, fully pure. Only with openness will the outside match the inside."

"We can demolish every deceptive fantasy that opposes God and break through every arrogant attitude that is raised up in defiance of the true knowledge of God. We capture, like prisoners of war, every thought and insist that it bow in obedience to the Anointed One."
2 Corinthians 10:5 TPT

"When our inner narrative is negative, we're under the influence of a lie. We're no longer controlling our story; it's controlling us. When our thoughts are dominated by anxiety and fear of the future, we are being ruled by that anxiety and fear. So, what do you do? Challenge every thought. Write them down and investigate them later when you have quiet time. In this introspection, find the truth and comfort that comes in the presence of Jesus."

"Don't fret or worry. Instead of worrying, pray. Let petitions and praises shape your worries into prayers, letting God know your concerns. Before you know it, a sense of God's wholeness, everything coming together for good, will come and settle you down. It's wonderful what happens when Christ displaces worry at the center of your life."
Philippians 4:6-7 MSG

"Your destiny is not to stay on the ground like a chicken but, rather, to see above the clouds like an eagle—from a higher perspective. You are called to soar!"

"You satisfy my every desire with good things. You've supercharged my life so that I soar again like a flying eagle in the sky!"
Psalm 103:5 TPT

"The more you understand whose you are, the more you can become the best version of who you were made to be."

"If we accept the testimony of men, how much more should we accept the more authoritative testimony of God that he has testified concerning his Son?"
1 John 5:9 TPT

"You were created with a purpose. There is destiny written in your heart. Don't waste your purpose out of fear of rejection, fear of embarrassment, or just plain carelessness. You matter, and you're worth it."

"A dear friend will love you no matter what, and a family sticks together through all kinds of trouble."
Proverbs 17:17 TPT

"The more you choose to be in His presence, the more you will recognize the Father's tone—kind, gentle, comforting, and always good. If you hear a voice that doesn't match, it's not Him speaking."

"Now, this is the goal: to live in harmony with one another and demonstrate affectionate love, sympathy, and kindness toward other believers. Let humility describe who you are as you dearly love one another."
1 Peter 3:8 TPT

"If, in every decision, we are asking, 'What is it going to cost me?', then self-gratification is at the core of our belief system. Everything comes back to: 'What's in it for me?' This will get you to a certain point of success in your life, but if you're looking to leave a legacy, then your motivation needs to shift from 'What's in it for me?' to 'What's in me that I can give away?'"

"Don't set the affections of your heart on this world or in loving the things of the world. The love of the Father and the love of the world are incompatible. For all that the world can offer us—the gratification of our flesh, the allurement of the things of the world, and the obsession with status and importance—none of these things come from the Father but from the world. This world and its desires are in the process of passing away, but those who love to do the will of God live forever."

1 John 2:15-17 TPT

"STOP dwelling on the doubts and 'what-ifs.' LOOK up to heaven in prayer instead. LISTEN for God's guidance. If we remove the distractions, we'll hear Him speak more clearly. Stop, look, and listen."

"Yes, feast on all the treasures of the heavenly realm and fill your thoughts with heavenly realities, and not with the distractions of the natural realm."
Colossians 3:2 TPT

"Don't fear confrontation. Although it can be uncomfortable, healthy confrontation will bring more truth into relationships than casual cover up conversations ever could."

"My beloved friends, if you see a believer who is overtaken with a fault, may the one who overflows with the Spirit seek to restore him. Win him over with gentle words, which will open his heart to you and will keep you from exalting yourself over him."
Galatians 6:1 TPT

"What does stewarding our conviction look like? Obedience, even when it's uncomfortable. Walking in freedom comes at a cost, but is the cost really as costly as we thought?"

"But those who love the truth will come out into the Light and welcome its exposure, for the Light will reveal that their fruitful works were produced by God."
John 3:21 TPT

"We don't have to rewrite the book of our lives. Just stay within the boundaries of His process. He has already written your story."

"I delight to fulfill your will, my God, for your living words are written upon the pages of my heart."
Psalm 40:8 TPT

"Give away your resources. Give away encouragement. Give away acts of service. The more you give into this way of living, the more empowerment you'll find in your life. Purpose will start to grow. Confidence will spark in your instinct to follow through on that random, risky thought. Go for it. You might change a life. You might change your life."

"He's informed us of the many wonderful ways love is being demonstrated through your lives by the empowerment of the Holy Spirit."
Colossians 1:8 TPT

"Build on what God has revealed in you. Use His truth as your foundation."

"Beloved, now we are children of God; and it has not yet been revealed what we shall be, but we know that when He is revealed, we shall be like Him, for we shall see Him as He is."
I John 3:2 NKJV

**"Trust Him more.
Ask Him more."**

"I've poured out my life before you, and you've always been there for me. So now I ask: teach me more of your holy decrees."
Psalm 119:26 TPT

"Some say, 'Check yourself before you wreck yourself.' I say, 'Check your heart before you wreck your heart.' The more you're aware of your present state of mind, the more you can sense, see and understand what is yours and what is not."

"So, here's what I've concluded. I will pray in the Spirit, but I will also pray with my mind engaged. I will sing rapturous praises in the Spirit, but I will also sing with my mind engaged."
1 Corinthians 14:15 TPT

"Honor God's timeline. Honor His process. Rest in knowing that He has you covered."

"As we enter into God's faith-rest life we cease from our own works, just as God celebrates his finished works and rests in them."
Hebrews 4:10 TPT

"Spiritual investments do not always get the fanfare our pride desires. But when you shift your perspective toward the Father, and your motivation toward bringing glory to God, your desire will change. Money is not the root of all evil, but the love of money is. Keep loving Him, and all other things will fall into place."

"To all the rich of this world, I command you not to be wrapped in thoughts of pride over your prosperity, or rely on your wealth, for your riches are unreliable and nothing compared to the living God. Trust instead in the one who lavishes upon us all good things, fulfilling our every need. Remind the wealthy to be rich in remarkable works of extravagant generosity, willing to share with others. These spiritual investments will provide a beautiful foundation for their lives and secure for them a great future, as they lay their hands upon the meaning of true life."

1 Timothy 6:17-19 TPT

"People of honor are people that honor their word. Let your 'yes' be 'yes.' Be someone who follows through."

"A beautiful reputation is more to be desired than great riches, and to be esteemed by others is more honorable than to own immense investments."
Proverbs 22:1 TPT

"Are we possessing or just professing? Are you just claiming why you know what you know or are you collaborating with the Spirit of love, word and deed?"

"It is my honor and constant passion to be a pioneer who preaches where no one has ever even heard of the Anointed One, instead of building upon someone else's foundation. As the Scriptures say: Those who know nothing about him will clearly see him, and those who have not heard will respond."
Romans 15:20-21 TPT

"So many people love the sun. It warms us, bronzes our skin and hides our flaws. If only we could see the Son of the Most High that way—the One who brings true warmth to the hearts of men. But instead of hiding our weaknesses, He brings the sins of our heart to light so true healing can take place."

"The word from heaven will come to us with dazzling light to shine upon those who live in darkness, near death's dark shadow. And he will illuminate the path that leads to the way of peace."
Luke 1:79 TPT

"Our atmosphere affects how we see things. Have the storms of our lives fogged your perspective? Keep persevering; when the fog evaporates, you'll be left with clarity. Trust God's timing, and, if all else fails, look up. The Son is always watching."

"While we anticipate and help to speed up the coming of the day of God, when the atmosphere will be set on fire and the heavenly bodies consumed in a blaze."
2 Peter 3:12 TPT

"Winter embraces resting. Spring embraces new life. Summer embraces warmth and growth. Fall embraces letting go. The seasons of our lives don't always move as quickly as the seasons of nature, but the concept still applies. If you don't know which season you are in, take a moment to ask your heart. It will allow you to pray more specific prayers. Surrender and settle into the seasons you are in and ask God what He wants to teach you in this season."

"Be cheerful with joyous celebration in every season of life. Let joy overflow, for you are united with the Anointed One!"
Philippians 4:4 TPT

"He knows my name. He knows every hair on my head. He knows the days ahead."

"Are not five sparrows sold for two copper coins? And not one of them is forgotten before God. But the very hairs of your head are all numbered. Do not fear therefore; you are of more value than many sparrows."
Luke 12:6-7 NKJV

"His glory is all around us. His blood is running through us."

"God's glory is all around me! His wrap-around presence is all I need, for the Lord is my Savior, my hero, and my life-giving strength."
Psalm 62:7 TPT

"When life slaps you in the face, it's time to own your moment. Through Jesus' work on the cross, the Holy Spirit living inside of you and the Father calling you His child, you have all you need to own your moment. You will prove who He is and who He has made you to be."

"Lord God, unlock my heart, unlock my lips, and I will overcome with my joyous praise!"
Psalm 51:15 TPT

"Instead of viewing heartbreak as hopeless, view it as a chance to surrender. There are seasons to allow our hearts to be broken so the Father can re-mend them."

"Laying your life down in tender surrender before the Lord will bring life, prosperity, and honor as your reward."
Proverbs 22:4 TPT

"Many roads we travel down in life have detours, road blocks, construction, and speed bumps along the way. All these are for our safety. They seem frustrating in the moment, but their purpose is to protect us and get us home safely. The same is true about the heart. The road might be narrow and challenging, but wholeness, freedom, and breakthrough are found at the end of this road."

"But small is the gate and narrow and difficult
to travel is the path that leads the way to
[everlasting] life, and there are few who find it."
Matthew 7:14 AMP

"The more we see His everyday gifts, the less we are consumed by our everyday burdens."

"True love for God means obeying his commands, and his commands don't weigh us down as heavy burdens."
1 John 5:3 TPT

"A surrendered heart to a good, good Father can never be broken because it's handled with care."

"Be enthusiastic to serve the Lord, keeping your passion toward him boiling hot! Radiate with the glow of the Holy Spirit and let him fill you with excitement as you serve him."
Romans 12:11 TPT

"It's not just a rhythm—it's His rhythm that was gifted to you in every heartbeat."

"Break forth with dancing! Make music and sing God's praises with the rhythm of drums!"
Psalm 149:3 TPT

"You're searching to find the lies within. Once the lies have been illuminated, it's time to start the work of renewal by replacing them with the truth. Once the truth has been planted, it needs time to become acquainted with your heart."

"So, keep your thoughts continually fixed on all that is authentic and real, honorable and admirable, beautiful and respectful, pure and holy, merciful and kind. And fasten your thoughts on every glorious work of God, praising him always."
Philippians 4:8 TPT

"Honor is something that used to be respected in our culture. Now it seems we are more about individual empowerment – every person for themselves. A culture of honor in the workplace is something that takes time to cultivate, but when employees see their fearless leader believes in them and empowers them to succeed, success becomes tangible and imminent."

"Instruct every employee to respect and honor
their employers, for this attitude presents to them
a clear testimony of God's truth and renown.
Tell them to never provide them with a reason to
discredit God's name because of their actions."
1 Timothy 6:1 TPT

"Sacrifice is a step beyond convenience. When you decide to sacrifice for someone else rather than receive for yourself, you are becoming a new creation. One surrendered sacrifice at a time creates a heart of service. Fulfillment is found in the arms of a heart surrendered to Christ."

"For the source of your pleasure is not in my performance or the sacrifices I might offer to you. The fountain of your pleasure is found in the sacrifice of my shattered heart before you. You will not despise my tenderness as I humbly bow down at your feet."
Psalm 51:16-17 TPT

"There is a saying: 'Let's get down to the heart of the matter.' Fearful thoughts are not inherently bad. We can channel those fears into a conversation with our hearts. As you ponder the source of those fears, understanding will come through the Spirit. Clarity will come as you seek to find truth in Christ."

"Let every word you speak be drenched with grace and tempered with truth and clarity. For then you will be prepared to give a respectful answer to anyone who asks about your faith."
Colossians 4:6 TPT

"He promises to never leave us nor forsake us. It's not just a verse; it's a promise. The more willing we are to dialogue with our innermost thoughts, the more open the door becomes to access the truths locked up inside. The more we know, the more we grow. "

"Don't be obsessed with money but live content with what you have, for you always have God's presence. For hasn't he promised you, 'I will never leave you alone, never! And I will not loosen my grip on your life!'"
Hebrews 13:5 TPT

"Your loving kindness is all around us. Through every battle, You are still in control."

"Her teachings are filled with wisdom and kindness
as loving instruction pours from her lips."
Proverbs 31:26 TPT

"When trials happen—grief, divorce, job loss, death of a loved one—the weight of these moments can make one feel they are sinking deep. Who can pull us out? Can we truly tell someone our inner thoughts? The Father above wants to hear every thought we have. His son came down from heaven 2,000 years ago, sacrificed Himself, and conquered the shame of all mankind. This is something to celebrate no matter the loss. The cross crushed the shame of sin within."

"For the arrows of your conviction have pierced me deeply. Your blows have struck my soul and crushed me."
Psalm 38:2 TPT

"Who is in control of your life? Often our lives are a push-and-pull inside of us to determine who is leading. Take some time today to ask your heart who's holding first place in your heart. It might surprise you."

"Guide me in your truth, and teach me, my God, my Savior. I trust you all day long."
Psalm 25:5 TPT

"Are you known for being a hothead? People follow those who are calm in the midst of pressure. Pressure can burst pipes. When you are self-aware, you learn to channel that energy toward positive outcomes. Don't fear the tension because it will help you find out what you are made of."

"An impulsive person has a short fuse and can ruin everything, but the wise show self-control."
Proverbs 14:17 TPT

"Self-pity means excessive, self-absorbed unhappiness in the midst of our troubles. When our self becomes our main focus, we can develop tunnel vision. It's better to acknowledge a higher power and invite Him into our moments of pity. When we surrender our weakness, we have access to a higher perspective."

"So, I'm not defeated by my weakness, but delighted! For when I feel my weakness and endure mistreatment—when I'm surrounded with troubles on every side and face persecution because of my love for Christ—I am made yet stronger. For my weakness becomes a portal to God's power."
2 Corinthians 12:10 TPT

"When we know whose voice is the right one to follow, it becomes that much easier to live out a life of purpose."

"Whoever serves me must follow me. Then my servant will be with me everywhere I am. My Father will honor anyone who serves me."
John 12:26 NCV

"As a parent, we find ourselves comparing our children to the external performance of others. What would change if we started to focus more on their spiritual gifts? The Father doesn't measure the same way we do. He measures by the fruits of the Holy Spirit we produce within our heart. As parents, let's make sure we are putting value on the things that last. Our children listen to us—what we say matters. Measure their joy. Measure their kindness. Don't simply measure their grades and sport wins. They need to be praised for more than their performance."

"Dedicate your children to God and point them in the way that they should go, and the values they've learned from you will be with them for life."
Proverbs 22:6 TPT

"Have you ever felt like you were walking blindly—going through life without feeling like you are making progress? In this world, there is a lot of darkness. We must become children of the light."

"Then Jesus said, 'The light will be with you for a little longer, so walk while you have the light. Then the darkness will not catch you. If you walk in the darkness, you will not know where you are going. Believe in the light while you still have it so that you will become children of light.' When Jesus had said this, he left and hid himself from them."

John 12:35-36 NCV

"Who holds your worth? God sees you as the most valuable thing in the world. You matter. You hold so much value. You are enough to Him, just the way you are."

"What is the value of your soul to God? Could your worth be defined by an amount of money? God doesn't abandon or forget even the small sparrow he has made. How then could he forget or abandon you? What about the seemingly minor issues of your life? Do they matter to God? Of course they do! So you never need to worry, for you are more valuable to God than anything else in this world."
Luke 12:6-7 TPT

"It's often said that God doesn't want to hear about my day when He has war, famine, and natural disaster to handle. Psalm 141:1-2 contradicts that idea. God loves to hear our prayers—it represents a relationship of dialogue. Sweet incense! What a beautiful picture. He desires to hear my voice, and when I come with praise and adoration, it's a sweet smell to His heart."

"GOD, come close. Come quickly! Open your ears—it's my voice you're hearing! Treat my prayer as sweet incense rising; my raised hands are my evening prayers."
Psalm 141:1-2 MSG

"Generosity is something you steward over time. When the thought comes to bless, follow through. Test Him on these things. Generosity is a boomerang—the more you give, the more abounding blessings come back in return. We don't give to get. We give to posture our hearts in surrendered obedience to He who gives us all we need."

"Learn to generously share what you have with those who ask for help, and don't close your heart to the one who comes to borrow from you."
Matthew 5:42 TPT

"Think how much God has given us freely. What if we had a spirit of giving within our hearts and minds—freely giving to those around us? We serve a Father who gives the best gifts. In the Kingdom of God, the supplies never run out. So, give like you have access to an endless supply from Heaven because you do! Wisdom is necessary in when to give, so listen to and partner with the Holy Spirit. If you are open to listening, He will speak to you as to whom and how much to give. Take a risk. The fulfillment inside grows with every act of obedience."

"Every gift God freely gives us is good and perfect, streaming down from the Father of lights, who shines from the heavens with no hidden shadow or darkness and is never subject to change."
James 1:17 TPT

"Praise and gratitude will change the narrative of your mind and heart. The more you praise God through the storm, the more you develop the perspective to see what is truly happening. You start to focus on what is all around you instead of all you have lost."

"He said: "I was naked when I was born, and I will be naked when I die. The LORD gave these things to me, and he has taken them away. Praise the name of the LORD."
Job 1:21 NCV

"Sometimes the loads we carry can seem too heavy to bear. We can start to resent the responsibilities of this life. Take heart. Joy and laughter are your portion. Armloads of blessings are around the corner for those who carry on."

"They may weep as they go out carrying their seed to sow, but they will return with joyful laughter and shouting with gladness as they bring back armloads of blessing and a harvest overflowing!"
Psalm 126:6 TPT

"In every season, joy is available. Maintaining this joy is key to holding on to the revelation of our salvation."

"I cried aloud to him with all my heart and he answered me! Now my mouth overflows with the highest praise."
Psalm 66:17 TPT

"It doesn't matter what I've done. It doesn't matter what I've seen. All that matters is what we glean in the between."

"Be committed to teach the believers all these things when you are with them in the presence of the Lord. Instruct them to never be drawn into meaningless arguments, or tear each other down with useless words that only harm others."
2 Timothy 2:14 TPT

"Do you have a close friend? Someone you can tell anything to and feel no shame or guilt? Can you count on them to be there no matter the circumstances? Yes, His name is Jesus! You can imagine you are riding on his shoulders when you tell him about your day. The more you embrace this dialogue with Jesus, the more you feel His presence, and the more you receive His presents."

"A man who has friends must himself be friendly, but there is a friend who sticks closer than a brother."
Proverbs 18:24 NKJV

"Have you ever thought that you are stuck in the middle of the storm? It doesn't feel comfortable but take heart—grace can be accessed in the middle. The lie is that you are alone in the middle, and the resolve is that He is always in the middle with you, willing and able to help."

"And led his people right through the middle! His tender love for us continues on forever!"
Psalm 136:14 TPT

"When the time comes to close the chapter of yesterday, look for the open doors around you. They may be small beginnings, but each door you walk through is big to God. It is faith in action."

"I know your works. See, I have set before you an open door, and no one can shut it; for you have a little strength, have kept My word, and have not denied My name."
Revelation 3:8 NKJV

"The more you know Jesus and His Word, the more confident you are in sowing into others."

"For when they observe your pure, godly life before God, it will impact them deeply."
1 Peter 3:2 TPT

"Looking for a way to change your attitude? Name three things that annoy you to no end. Next name three things that bless you above all. The blessings always outweigh the negatives. Your attitude tells more about your being than anything else. Stay grateful."

"Lord, receive my grateful thanks and teach me more of how to please you."
Psalm 119:108 TPT

"What do you want? What do you need? Two questions, you can ask yourself. These two questions can also lead into a lot of conversations with people. When was the last time someone asked you what you truly want? So many times, we just fulfill the duties of what we think people need. Without actually asking them "Is this truly something you need?" Asking someone else what they need makes you vulnerable, but it shows you care about meeting their need more than your self-satisfaction."

"Your surplus could meet their need, and their abundance may one day meet your need. This equal sharing of abundance will mean a fair balance."
2 Corinthians 8:14 TPT

"In the breaking comes an awakening!"

"Then may your awakening breath blow upon my life until I am fully yours. Breathe upon me with your Spirit wind. Stir up the sweet spice of your life within me. Spare nothing as you make me your fruitful garden. Hold nothing back until I release your fragrance. Come walk with me as you walked with Adam in your paradise garden. Come taste the fruits of your life in me. I have come to you, my darling bride, for you are my paradise garden! Come walk with me until I am fully yours. Come taste the fruits of your life in me."

Song of Songs 4:16 TPT

"The promise becomes a place, and the place becomes a home. There we will find our peace, and in that home our love is the treasure that ties us together."

"In My Father's house are many mansions; if it were not so, I would have told you. I go to prepare a place for you."
John 14:2 NKJV

"When a kind word from a sweet-spirited heart is communicated, it will warm someone's heart and mend their soul. Be the sweet spirit today."

"Be faithful to guard the sweet harmony of the Holy Spirit among you in the bonds of peace, being one body and one spirit, as you were all called into the same glorious hope of divine destiny. For the Lord God is one, and so are we, for we share in one faith, one baptism, and one Father. And He is the perfect Father who leads us all, works through us all, and lives in us all!"
Ephesians 4:3-6 TPT

"He desires us to stay connected no matter the circumstances. It may not be the answer we wanted or thought, but God knows what we need. Allow grace to come in to your life so acceptance can be your portion. This is the day that the Lord has made, I will rejoice and be glad in it. The start of a good day includes believing God knows best for us. Stand faithful, my friend."

"So you must be sure to keep the message burning in your hearts; that is, the message of life you heard from the beginning. If you do, you will always be living in close fellowship with the Son and with the Father."
1 John 2:24 TPT

"Have you ever cried yourself to sleep? When fear is taking grip and the loneliness takes root, at this moment surrender and bow down and give it all to Jesus. He will wipe away every tear! No tear is lost with the Father. They have all been recorded. Take heart! The King cares about you."

"You've kept track of all my wandering and my weeping. You've stored my many tears in your bottle—not one will be lost. For they are all recorded in your book of remembrance."
Psalm 56:8 TPT

"Life has a way of hi-jacking our peace. Here are three things you may find helpful moving forward when different setbacks come your way: first, make sure you have a good support system; second, find a local church to keep you connected; third, keep telling the Father about your hopes and dreams. Start dreaming again because one day it may come true!"

"When hope's dream seems to drag on and on, the delay can be depressing. But when at last your dream comes true, life's sweetness will satisfy your soul."
Proverbs 13:12 TPT

"At times when you feel there is nowhere safe to go to be sad, stop, pause, and say, 'I know the Way, the Truth, and I have His life in me. Remember your position is sitting on His eternal shoulders and sharing your heart. So, when you feel there is no place safe to be sad, know that God is the place you go to be restored. In these moments of restoration, regeneration begins. Our Father, God, never gets tired of holding you up on His shoulders. He can hold this position until eternity, so rest in knowing He's got you by the hand."

"Turning to his servants, the father said, 'Quick, bring me the best robe, my very own robe, and I will place it on his shoulders. Bring the ring, the seal of sonship, and I will put it on his finger. And bring out the best shoes you can find for my son."

Luke 15:22 TPT

"Running this race called life looks different for each person. The length of stride is different. The cadence of their steps is different. We can't compare our race to another's. What are you running towards? Or are you running away from your yesterdays? I want to take a moment to encourage you, the reader, to never stop moving! Your race matters. Keep pressing towards your finish line. It might be a sprint or it might be a long-distance race. Life happens and we have to learn to roll with it and keep on stepping. We are running towards that great cloud of witnesses. Keep running into your destiny, into your purpose, into moments of togetherness, and into the happiest days of your life."

"As for us, we have all of these great witnesses who encircle us like clouds. So, we must let go of every wound that has pierced us and the sin we so easily fall into. Then we will be able to run life's marathon race with passion and determination, for the path has been already marked out before us."

Hebrews 12:1 TPT

"What is a treasure? Is it something you discover or find? Is it something you search for, pray for, or hope to find? It can be all of the above. So, ask yourself this one question, 'Will you treasure your treasure?' A wise person that discovers a treasure knows to cherish it. To protect it. To give into it. To show kindness to it. To breathe goodness into it. And finally, to be patient with it. When you find your treasure, you will know—and never doubt—that it is part of an eternal story."

"For your heart will always pursue what you value as your treasure."
Matthew 6:21 TPT